The
SUPREME
COURT

Troll Associates

The
SUPREME
COURT

by Rae Bains

Illustrated by Bob Dole

Troll Associates

Library of Congress Cataloging in Publication Data

Bains, Rae.
   Supreme Court.

   Summary: Explains the importance of the Supreme Court,
which interprets the Constitution and makes decisions
which establish precedents to guide all laws and legal
action in the country.
    1. United States. Supreme Court—Juvenile literature.
2. United States—Constitutional law—Juvenile literature.
[1. United States. Supreme Court. 2. United States—
Constitutional law. 3. Courts. 4. Law] I. Dole, Bob,
ill. II. Title.
KF8742.Z9B34   1985   347.73 '26   84-2736
ISBN 0-8167-0272-1 (lib. bdg.) 347.30735
ISBN 0-8167-0273-X (pbk.)

Early in the nineteenth century, the famous inventor, Robert Fulton, built a steamboat. Shortly afterward, the state of New York gave Fulton's company the sole right to run a steamboat service on the Hudson River, between New York and New Jersey. This made New Jersey boatmen angry because the river belonged to New Jersey as well as New York. The two states got into a legal battle over the situation.

The disagreement became one of the first major cases that finally reached the United States Supreme Court. Under the United States Constitution, the Supreme Court—the highest court in the country—has the power to decide legal conflicts between states.

In the Fulton case, Chief Justice John Marshall handed down a decision that ruled against the state of New York and in favor of the state of New Jersey.

The Supreme Court ruled that only the federal government could make laws on commerce between two or more states. Since a boat crossing the Hudson was involved in commerce between two states, neither New York nor New Jersey could give any company the sole right to use the Hudson River.

This decision, although it dealt only with one legal case, had a far-reaching effect. It set a *precedent* for all cases involving

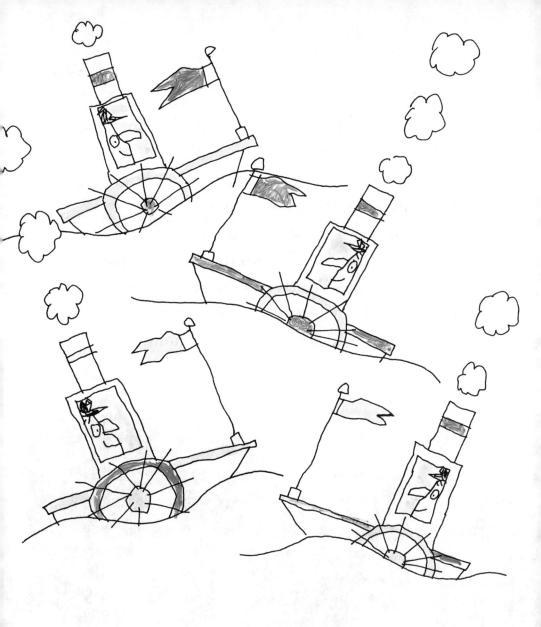

commerce between two or more states. A precedent is a decision made in one case which can be applied to all cases like it.

When the Supreme Court was established, nobody was sure how it would be run. The Constitution simply said that there would be one Supreme Court and some lower courts to be established by Congress.

These courts would deal with foreign treaties, foreign diplomats, naval affairs, controversies between states, between citizens of different states, and between Americans and foreign governments.

The Constitution didn't say how many judges would make up the Supreme Court, or how many lower courts there would be, or how the courts would operate, or how they would enforce their decisions.

Then the United States Congress made a law that set up the lower courts, the number of justices on the Supreme Court, how much they were to be paid, and so forth.

But exactly how the Supreme Court would operate didn't become clear until it began to hear actual cases. Then, year by year and case by case, the court began making history.

The Supreme Court is the final judge of what the Constitution means. Every time the Supreme Court has made a decision in its two-hundred-year history, it has established a precedent to guide all laws and legal action in the country.

For example, when George Washington, the first President of the United States, wanted legal advice on a proposed treaty, he asked the new Supreme Court for its opinion. The Constitution did not say whether the justices could or couldn't give such an opinion. But the justices said that they could not advise the President personally. They could only offer legal opinions on cases brought before them in a lawsuit.

This set a Supreme Court precedent. From then on, the court would offer no opinion except on matters contained in a lawsuit brought before it.

Another important precedent was set by the Supreme Court early in its history. This precedent was one of *judicial review.* This means that the court has the power to pass judgment on acts of Congress.

The Supreme Court can decide if a law passed by Congress is constitutional. If the court decides that a law violates the Constitution, the law must be thrown out. This power of judicial review has given the court great strength in American government.

When the founders of the United States set up the government, they created three branches. These were the executive, the legislative, and the judicial. This was done so that no single person or group would be able to take control of the country. These three branches would balance each other and keep a check on each other's power.

The Constitution spelled out the powers of Congress and the President. But it didn't spell out the powers of the Supreme Court. And the court might not have become an equal branch of U.S. government without the power of judicial review.

For example, the Constitution guarantees freedom of speech. But suppose that Congress passes a law forbidding all red-headed persons to speak on any subject in a public place.

This law is clearly against the Constitution. And obviously some redheaded person will eventually break this law and be tried in a court of law. If the person is convicted, and if he or she appeals the verdict, the case may eventually reach the United States Supreme Court.

The redhead can claim that the law under which he or she was convicted is unconstitutional. And the Supreme Court would surely agree and throw out that law. Simply knowing that judicial review exists helps to keep Congress from passing laws that are unreasonable or unconstitutional.

In the same way, the Supreme Court has been a balancing force against unreasonable acts by Presidents. One United States President tried to take over a whole industry to prevent a strike. The Supreme Court ruled that the President had gone beyond the powers given that office by the Constitution.

When another President claimed that he had a special right to withhold evidence needed in a criminal trial, the Supreme Court ruled against him. In these ways, the highest court has made it clear to all Presidents that they are not above the law.

Because its decisions carry such weight, the court takes care not to act too quickly or in any extreme way. The court may take months to hear the arguments in an important case, to discuss the issues of the case, and to write a decision.

Every year thousands of cases are filed in the hope that the court will hear them. Most of the cases filed for consideration are refused by the court. This is called "denying a petition." The nine justices who make up the court may deny a petition because it is not important enough. The Supreme Court may also deny a petition because it is hearing a similar case or has just ruled on a similar case.

Even so, the Supreme Court, sitting in Washington, D.C., hears thousands of cases during each term. A term begins on the first Monday in October and usually ends the next summer. But this doesn't mean that the Supreme Court justices aren't working between terms. Many important decisions have been written between terms and announced on the first Monday in October, when the court begins its new term.

When the Supreme Court grants a petition and agrees to consider a case, the justices read all the records of the case. Then they hear the legal arguments given by lawyers representing the two sides in the case.

These Supreme Court sessions are not like other court trials. There are no witnesses to be questioned and there is no jury. Also, the people who are personally involved in the case are not required to be present.

A Supreme Court hearing involves the justices and the lawyers, discussing points of law. The justices may ask questions at any time during the hearing, and they may ask for more information. Then they announce their decision.

Sometimes, all of the nine justices agree. It is said then that the decision is unanimous. Sometimes, the justices disagree. Then the majority rules. A Supreme Court decision may be 5-4, 6-3, 7-2, 8-1, or unanimous.

After the justices have voted in private on their decision, the chief justice names one justice to write the majority opinion, for which at least five justices have voted. The other justices are free to write individual opinions for or against the decision.

Sometimes, the Supreme Court decides that the decision of the lower courts should stand. This ends the matter. The Supreme Court may even overturn one of its own

rulings. One of the best examples of this concerns racial discrimination.

In 1896, the Supreme Court upheld a Louisiana law that separated black and white people using railway trains. The court ruled that this kind of segregation was constitutional as long as there were equal facilities for both blacks and whites. This ruling made segregation laws legal for many years.

Then, in the early 1950s, the Supreme Court agreed to hear a group of cases concerning racial segregation in public schools. And, in a historic decision, the nation's highest court ruled that segregation laws were unconstitutional. It was clear, the decision said, that any time there was racial separation of this kind, there was also inequality.

With this decision, and others like it, the Supreme Court overturned the rulings of earlier Supreme Courts. It also started a new chapter in American history, in which the constitutional guarantees of equality were extended to all Americans.

Over the years, the Supreme Court has come under criticism for different reasons. Some people believe the court is too slow to act. Some say it is old-fashioned. Others say it is too quick to call for change.

Yet in spite of these criticisms, the United States Supreme Court is the most reliable defender of justice that any nation has ever had.